BREEDERS' BEST
A KENNEL CLUB BOOK™

Dachshund

By Stephen Nappe

D1198568

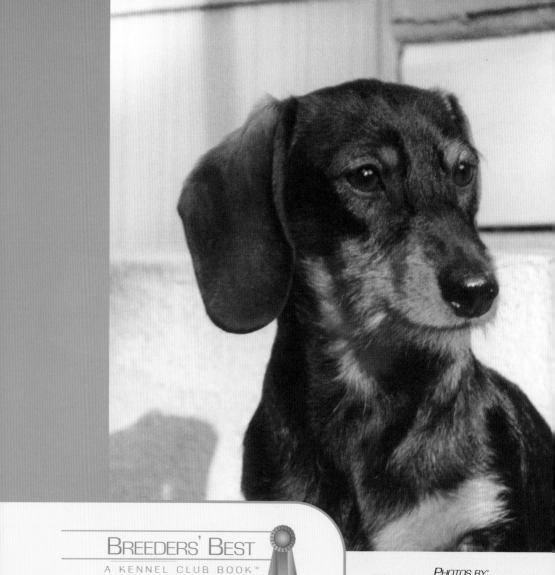

BREEDERS' BEST
A KENNEL CLUB BOOK™

DACHSHUND

ISBN: 1-59378-907-6

Copyright © 2004

Kennel Club Books, LLC
308 Main Street, Allenhurst, NJ 07711 USA
Printed in South Korea

PHOTOS BY:
Carla Aldarelli, Bernd Brinkman
Dorothy Eisele, Isabelle França
John Merriman, Stephen Napp
and Robert White.

DRAWINGS BY:
Elvira

Contents

CHAPTER 1

Meet the Dachshund

The Dachshund hails from Germany, where the name translates as "badger dog." This indeed was one of the breed's tasks, but by no means was this its only function.

To begin, we must look back in time to the many centuries during which much of Europe was forestland, when the majority of dogs used for the hunt were large. As time progressed, deforestation increased and the huntsmen needed

A handsome trio from Germany, the breed's homeland, in which the Dachshund is called *Teckel*.

a wider variety of hound types to aid them. By the 16th century, shorter-legged dogs with somewhat longer bodies and long, pendant ears had been developed. These were by no means as small as the Dachshunds we know today, but they were undoubtedly their predecessors.

A Miniature on the prowl. The Dachshund in all of its varieties is an effective "badger dog" and hunter of small vermin.

Different European countries developed their smaller hounds along different lines according to the needs of the huntsmen of each particular area. Those in France primarily became the dogs we know today as the various "basset" breeds, including the Basset Hound, Petit Basset Griffon Vendéen and Basset Fauve de Bretagne.

In Germany and some of the surrounding districts, people needed a robust hound that was sufficiently small to work its way through dense undergrowth. This hound also needed a good nose that he could use for

The wirehaired coat provides protection for the dog while he is at work in the field and brush.

hunting and for tracking wounded game. The hound needed to give tongue as he barked to give notice to the hunters of the prey's whereabouts, but the dog was not required to attack. The hound had to be sufficiently small to move at the same pace as the hunters, who traveled either on foot or on relatively short-legged horses.

So the Dachshund developed to fill these needs. The breed became principally renowned for its hunting and tracking skills. It did, of course, also go to ground, as the name "badger dog" implies, and there is no doubt that the Dachshund was also useful in controlling badgers and other vermin that were overly plentiful.

In the 16th century, there seem to have been two main types: those with smooth, short hair and crooked legs, others that were wire haired with straight legs. Until 1685, when the actual name "Dachshund" appeared in a book, various names had been used, among them "burrow dog," "earth dog," "badger creeper" and *bibarhund*," meaning "beaver dog."

By the 18th century, Dachshunds were described as being "the dwarfs of all other dogs," with their short legs "somewhat bent." Among other colors, dapples with a wall eye (a wholly or partly colored light-blue eye) were known from early times, and those described as "striped tiger" were highly prized. White patches on the throat and chest were not considered desirable. During this time, most Dachshunds were owned by the nobility but lived with the foresters in their cottages, generally in small packs of just four or five.

As the 19th century dawned, the Dachshund was still active in Germany. In the all-breed stud book of 1840, 54 Dachshunds appeared, and the breed's first standard of points was drawn up in 1879. An early famous breeder was Wilhelm von Daake, who believed an ideal weight for the breed to be about 16 lb, but he admitted to having difficulty in keeping their weights below 20 lb.

Because they appear in early woodcuts, it is likely that longhaired Dachshunds had long existed in the breed, even though they were less popular. There is also a possibility that a longhaired gundog, rather like the Münsterländer, played a part in this variety's development. It was not until 1882 that a Dachshund of the longhaired variety appeared at a show in Hanover, but it was generally thought to have been the result of a cross between a smooth Dachshund and a spaniel.

The Deutscher Teckelklub was founded in 1880, with a special stud book for the breed commencing in 1890. This breed club plays a very important part in the breed in Germany to this day, and has set down strict rules not only for breeding Dachshund but also for hunting trials, tracking and going to ground.

The longhair is not the coat type most commonly seen, but this variety is known to have existed well before its first appearance in the show ring in 1882 in Germany.

In England, Dachshunds caught the public's attention in the first half of the 19th century, when they were owned by Queen Victoria and Prince Albert. The prince used his Dachshunds to drive the birds when he was shooting pheasant.

There was much discussion as to whether the breed was a hound or a terrier, and several authoritative 19th-century canine works classify the Dachshund as the latter. This may be because the breed was mistakenly thought to have been originally developed only to go to ground.

It was in 1870 that a Dachshund first appeared at a show in England, with the first separate class for the breed following in 1873. In 1881, a small group of gentlemen, each of whom had sizable kennels, got together to form the UK's Dachshund Club.

In the United States, it was William Loeffler of Wisconsin, who had bought a dog and bitch from Germany's Duke of Coburg in 1879, who was the first to show a Dachshund in the country.

Obviously, World War I called a halt to exports, but both before and after the war, a good number of Dachshunds was exported both to Britain and to the US. However, the breed suffered from lack of popularity in Britain during World War II, though in the US it retained its high ranking. The dogs that had been exported were mostly smooths, but there were also a few long- and wirehaired Dachshunds. The wires had appeared in Germany quite early in the breed's history, when it is likely that the wire-haired pinscher was crossed

The Dachshund's first breed standard was drawn up in 1879. The breed is now known around the globe and is a popular show dog worldwide.

with the smooth Dachshund. This, however, produced a longer leg, so later the Dandie Dinmont Terrier was used to shorten leg length, though this brought with it the problem of softening the coat. Today's wirehaired Dachshund has a short, harsh outer coat with somewhat softer hairs in the undercoat, and of course those distinguished beard and brows!

Although Miniature Dachshunds had been seen regularly in Germany, where they were interbred with Standards, as indeed the different coat types were interbred, it was not until the 1920s that they took a hold, first in Britain and then in the US. In both countries, the Dachshund is shown only in two sizes, with three different coat types. Countries breeding and exhibiting under the rules of Europe's Fédération Cynologique Internationale (FCI) also have three coat types but have three different sizes: Dachshund (Teckel), Miniature Dachshund (Miniature Teckel) and Rabbit Dachshund (Rabbit Teckel), making nine varieties in all.

MEET THE DACHSHUND

Overview

- The Dachshund was developed to aid hunters in situations where the traditional hunting breeds were too large.
- The Dachshund has always been prized for his tracking and hunting skills, owned by royalty and the general public alike.
- Both smooth and wire Dachshunds can be traced back to at least the 1500s. The longhair emerged in the late 1800s, although evidence shows he existed long before his first show-ring appearance.
- Today, Dachshunds are seen in the US and UK in two sizes and three coat types; in most of Europe and elsewhere, there are three sizes and three coat types.

Description of the Dachshund

A great little character, with an extroverted personality and an ability to act the fool on occasion—that sums up the Dachshund for you! This faithful, friendly breed should never be nervous or aggressive, but is clever, lively and courageous to the point of rashness. The highly versatile Dachshund is a passionate and persevering hunting dog that can work both above and below ground. He has an excellent nose and is a good tracker.

A handsome wirehair, seen in black with tan markings. The Dachshund's three coat types can occur in many attractive colors and combinations.

Some Dachshunds are more extroverted than others, but the majority become especially attached to one particular member of the family. Their choice is usually based on with which person they spend the most time. They make great family dogs, especially the Standard variety. Standards are sturdier and more robust, and thus better able to withstand the lively play of children. Most Dachshunds love children, but adult supervision and sensible guidance are always necessary.

The longhaired coat type brings a touch of elegance to the breed in all of its various color possibilities.

Regardless of its size, everyone knows that a Dachshund is long and low. The American Kennel Club (AKC) divides Dachshunds into two sizes, Standard and Miniature, as does the English Kennel Club. The Standard, the larger of the two, usually weighs between 16 and 32 pounds (in the UK, up to 26 pounds.) Miniatures must weigh under 11 pounds, and dogs are weighed at each show in which they are entered to compete.

The rich red coloration, accentuated by the vibrant sheen of the smooth coat variety.

Dachshund

CORRECT	INCORRECT

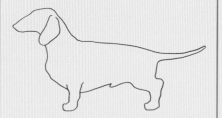

Body structure in profile.

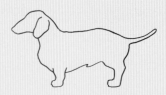

Dip behind shoulders, rise over loin, too much tuck-up.

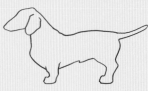

Sway back, too much tuck-up.

View of dog when moving away.

Turning out at hocks.   Cowhocks.

Straight, strong, parallel forelegs.

Legs set in too close.

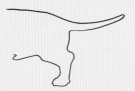

Proper tail set and carriage.

Tail set and carriage too low.   Tail set too high.

Size is measured very differently in the breed's homeland and other FCI countries. There are three size varieties in these countries: the Rabbit, the Miniature and the Standard. These countries determine the size of the two smaller varieties by the circumference of the dog's chest. From the age of 15 months, Miniatures measure 12 to 14 inches around the chest, and Rabbits up to 12 inches.

All Dachshunds are short-legged and of an elongated but compact build. Nonetheless, they are not restricted in movement, which must be free and flowing. The stride should be long, with drive from behind.

Because of the Dachshund's original function in life, the front assembly is strong deep and cleanly muscled, with the breastbone very prominent. The ribs are full and extend well back. Shoulders are well-laid-back, and the back is level. The tail is a continuation of the spine. It is only slightly curved, with no kinks or twists.

The rump is strong, with clean muscles and joints forming right angles. When seen from behind, the Dachshund's legs should be set well apart, straight and parallel. The front feet are full, broad, deep and close-knit, making them suitable for digging. They may point straight forward or can just slightly turn out. The hind feet are smaller, narrower and forward-pointing. A Dachshund must stand "true," meaning equally on all parts of the feet.

The head of the Dachshund is long and tapers uniformly to the tip of the nose. The ridges over the eyes are prominent; the stop is not. The muzzle is slightly arched. The medium-sized, almond-shaped eyes are energetic, giving a pleasant

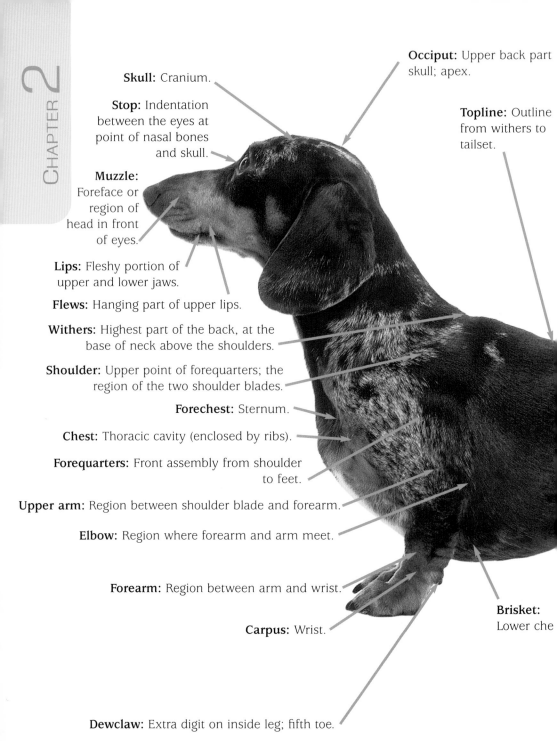

Skull: Cranium.

Occiput: Upper back part skull; apex.

Stop: Indentation between the eyes at point of nasal bones and skull.

Topline: Outline from withers to tailset.

Muzzle: Foreface or region of head in front of eyes.

Lips: Fleshy portion of upper and lower jaws.

Flews: Hanging part of upper lips.

Withers: Highest part of the back, at the base of neck above the shoulders.

Shoulder: Upper point of forequarters; the region of the two shoulder blades.

Forechest: Sternum.

Chest: Thoracic cavity (enclosed by ribs).

Forequarters: Front assembly from shoulder to feet.

Upper arm: Region between shoulder blade and forearm.

Elbow: Region where forearm and arm meet.

Forearm: Region between arm and wrist.

Brisket: Lower che

Carpus: Wrist.

Dewclaw: Extra digit on inside leg; fifth toe.

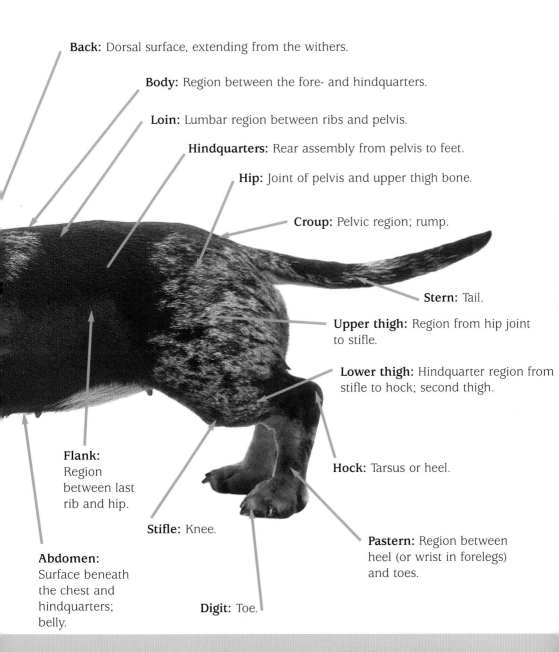

Back: Dorsal surface, extending from the withers.

Body: Region between the fore- and hindquarters.

Loin: Lumbar region between ribs and pelvis.

Hindquarters: Rear assembly from pelvis to feet.

Hip: Joint of pelvis and upper thigh bone.

Croup: Pelvic region; rump.

Stern: Tail.

Upper thigh: Region from hip joint to stifle.

Lower thigh: Hindquarter region from stifle to hock; second thigh.

Flank: Region between last rib and hip.

Hock: Tarsus or heel.

Stifle: Knee.

Pastern: Region between heel (or wrist in forelegs) and toes.

Abdomen: Surface beneath the chest and hindquarters; belly.

Digit: Toe.

expression. In most colors, they are dark, but can be lighter in chocolates. Wall eyes may be present in dappled dogs.

Complete dentition is important in the Dachshund. The teeth are powerful in a regular, scissor bite. The AKC considers an even bite to be a minor fault, but any other bite that deviates from the correct scissors bite is a serious fault.

Dachshunds' ears are set high and not too far forward. They are broad, of moderate length and well rounded, with the forward edge touching the cheek so that the ears frame the face.

There are three coat types for the Dachshund; which do you prefer? The smooth Dachshund has dense, short, smooth hair, with coarser hair on the underside of the tail. On smooths, the skin is loose and supple, but fits closely without dewlap, and little or no wrinkle.

The longhaired variety is equally attractive, with soft hair that is straight or only slightly waved. It is longest under the neck, on the underparts of the body, behind the legs and on the tail, where it forms a flag. The outside of the ears are well feathered, but there should not be too much hair on the feet.

Now we come to the wirehaired Dachshund, perhaps the most extroverted of all three! Except for the jaw, eyebrows, chin and ears, the whole body is covered with a short, straight, harsh coat, with a dense undercoat. The eyebrows are bushy, the ears almost smooth, and there is a beard on the chin. Legs and feet have a neat, harsh coat.

Dachshunds can be solid-colored in red (sometimes with sable markings) or cream, or two-colored in black, chocolate, wild boar, (or mixture of black, brown and gray), gray (blue) and fawn (Isabella), each with tan markings. Perhaps the most attractive coloration for the Dachshund is the dappled. As the AKC standard defines this unique color: "The 'single' dapple pattern is expressed as lighter-colored areas contrasting with the darker base color, which may be any acceptable color. A 'double' dapple is one in which varying amounts of white coloring occur over the body in addition to the dapple pattern." There are also brindles, with black or dark stripes over the whole body.

Except in dapples, which should be evenly marked all over, no white is permissible, except for a small patch on the chest, though this is not desirable. Nose and nails should be black in all colors except chocolate/tan and chocolate/dapple, where brown is permitted. For certain the Dachshund is a colorful breed, well fitting the lively character of this remarkable dog that finds it so easy to capture people's hearts.

A DESCRIPTION OF THE DACHSHUND

Overview

- The Dachshund is a well-rounded companion, possessing keen hunting ability, a plucky personality and a friendly nature.
- A breed standard is a document usually written by a national breed club, detailing the ideal characteristics of the breed in physical traits, abilities and temperament. Breed standards may vary from country to country, but each describe essentially the same dog.
- The Dachshund is seen in three coat varieties and two sizes: Standard and Miniature. In Europe, a third smaller size, Rabbit, is recognized. Many colors and patterns are seen.

Are You a Dachshund Person?

If you have a friendly personality, you and your Dachshund will immediately have something in common. Having a lively mind will also be an advantage, for your Dachshund is an intelligent companion with a strong character. Your Dachshund is quite capable of running rings around you if you are not quick-witted enough to keep up with him! You must make it clear to your dog that you are the boss, not him. You

Personality-packed Dachshunds delight their owners even when sleeping! Buzz thinks his friend Astrid makes a warm, cozy pillow and doesn't hesitate to cuddle up.

must never be unkind or harsh, but a commanding tone of voice will undoubtedly be an asset. You will need to train your dog to be obedient, and his training should start while he is still young. Additionally, hours of enjoyment will be spent watching your Dachshund clown around and, if you are willing to join in with his games, he will be that much happier.

The Dachshund is a small breed, and owners of all varieties find themselves fiercely devoted to the breed. It will be an advantage if you are fairly active, because as an adult your Dachshund will enjoy a good walk each day. Although small, he is energetic!

Note, however, that you will do your young puppy no favors if you exercise him for more than 20 minutes a day before he is about 6 months old. A Dachshund allowed to become bored can be destructive

From tenacious worker to huggable companion, the Dachshund has it all. Breeder Stephen Nappe gives Zin, a field champion, a lift.

Catching some rays! Zindox Steffi von Steiff is just lounging around on a sunny day.

around the home, not to mention noisy. If you are a house-proud person, or if you want to keep on good terms with your neighbors, or both, you will make sure that your Dachshund gets his exercise!

The house-proud owner will be interested to know that wirehairs do not shed coat around the home, but they will need to be stripped (a method of coat care done with a stripping knife or a well-trained thumb). This is quite an art if you want your dog to look his best. You may prefer to have a professional groomer do this or at least show you the correct way.

Martini and Rigatoni pose with a proud grandmother, Dolly Aldarelli.

Because yours is a small dog, you don't need a particularly large home. If you live in an apartment, you will be glad to know that you can still thoroughly enjoy your lives together, provided you don't neglect to go out for regular walks. No Dachshund will benefit from living on the 44th floor of a city walk-up, so think *elevator* when you go apartment shopping.

If you have a well-manicured lawn or landscaped garden surrounding your home, take heed. The Dachshund is a great digger and also a clever escape artist, so you will need to spend plenty of time outdoors, checking every little nook and cranny. In Germany, Dachshunds are measured by the circumference of their chests, indicating how small a hole they can fit through. Keep that in mind when your Dachshund is burrowing his way under your chain-link fence! I hope you will also have the good sense to put up "close the gate" signs, because your Dachshund will be off in a flash if a visitor is unthoughtful enough to leave your gate open.

As a caring owner, you will always take into consideration that your Dachshund is quite differently shaped than the majority of other breeds. You will therefore not allow him to jump from high places or to climb stairs, so as to avoid the danger of back injury. When you pick him up, you will always remember to support his back.

Should there be children in your home, you must be a sensible parent, who will teach them to respect your diminutive Dachshund. No dog is a plaything. He will enjoy games with all of you, but you must all use common sense and care.

Just as your children look to you for guidance, so will your Dachshund look to you for security. If you are devoted to your Dachshund, that is something else you will have in common, because if you treat him kindly and look after him well, he will almost certainly be absolutely devoted to you.

ARE YOU A DACHSHUND PERSON?

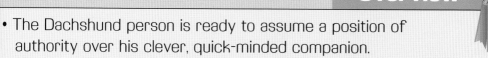

Overview

- The Dachshund person is ready to assume a position of authority over his clever, quick-minded companion.
- The Dachshund person is commited to caring for and exercising his dog, as is fortunate that the breed's small size makes him adaptable to almost any living environment.
- The Dachshund person appreciates a dog who will be as devoted to him as he is to the dog.
- The Dachshund person always puts his dog's safety first and make sure the gate is closed and the fence is secure.

Selecting a Dachshund Breeder

First, you will have come to a decision as to which of the three coat types you would like your "Dachshund-to-be" to have. Then, you will have to decide which size you prefer. These things done, you will be in a position to narrow down the list of Dachshund breeders to those who specialize in your desired variety. In the US, there are six possible combinations; in Europe, there are nine! Never rush into buying a puppy too hastily. If you have to wait a while to get the puppy

Breeders Stephen Nappe and Dorothy Eisele of Zindox Miniature Dachshunds with one of their wirehairs.

you want, then so be it. The wait will be well worthwhile.

Prospective puppy buyers should always keep foremost in their minds that there are many different kinds of breeder, some with the breed's interest at heart, others less dedicated. It is essential that you locate one that has not only dogs you admire but also breeding ethics with which you can agree. Sadly, in all breeds, there are invariably some who are simply "in it for the money," and these you must give a wide berth.

The aim of every breeder should be to pass on soundness, good health and the best characteristics of the Dachshund to each generation.

Recently, the author happened upon a poster in a local pizzeria, advertising "Datsons for Sale!" Apparently, some local "breeder" was selling two remaining puppies from a random litter. A good rule of thumb when selecting a breeder is to be sure that the breeder can spell the name of the breed!

Established breeders, those who have experience in the breed, do not

One of the best places to make contacts is a dog show. Once their turn in the ring is over, approach the handlers of the dogs that you like to get breeder referrals and other information.

advertise in newspapers or on the bulletin board of the neighborhood eatery. With a breed as structurally unique as the Dachshund, you are well advised to find a breeder who has the requisite knowledge and experience to breed sound dogs and raise a healthy litter.

There are many good breeders around and, if you look carefully, you will find just such a person. The AKC and Dachshund Club of America are trusted sources from which to find referrals. Once you contact a breeder, you still need to be sure that his standards of care are what you expect. You must also be certain that the breeder fully understands the breed and gives careful consideration to every mating, taking into consideration the dogs' pedigrees and health.

The breeder you select may be someone who breeds from home, in which case the puppies should have been brought up in the house and will be familiar with all the activities and noise of the daily routine. However, the breeder may run a larger establishment in which the litter has perhaps been raised in a kennel situation. Still, if you have chosen wisely, the puppies will have had lots of exposure to various sounds and sights of the breeder and his family. Even some of the larger breeding establishments whelp litters inside the home, and in my personal opinion this is infinitely better than puppies' being raised entirely in a kennel environment, especially for small breeds such as the Dachshund.

However large or small the breeding establishment, it is important that the conditions in which the puppies are raised are suitable. The areas should be clean and the puppies should be well supervised in a suitable environment. All pups should

If the breeder has children in the family, the pups will be accustomed to young people before they leave for new homes, which is a great benefit to new owners in their socialization efforts.

CHAPTER 4

look in tiptop condition. Their temperaments should be sound, and they should be full of fun, with plenty of confidence. However, if you take children along to visit the litter, you must take care that they are very gentle and do not frighten the puppies with

how she interacts with her offspring. If the dam is not available for you to see, be warned that this might be a sign that the puppies were not born on the premises, but were brought in from elsewhere to be sold. This is far from ideal!

Many breeders truly give a big part of their lives and homes to the breed that they love. Take the time to meet all of the dogs on the breeder's premises, as this is a wonderful way to see how the breeder cares for his dogs and how dogs of his line mature.

loud noises or quick, unexpected actions.

The breeder should be perfectly willing to show you the dam, and it will be interesting for you to take careful note of her temperament and

As for the stud dog, it is likely that he will not be available, for he may well be owned by someone else. A careful breeder may have traveled a great distance to use his stud services. Nonetheless, dedicated breeders will be able to show you at least a picture of the sire and his pedigree, as well as tell you about him.

A well-chosen breeder is able to give new puppy owners much useful guidance, including advice about feeding. Some breeders give a small quantity of puppy food to new owners when the puppies leave for new homes. In any event, the breeder should always provide written details of exactly what type and quantity of food have been fed, and with what

regularity. You will, of course, be able to change this as time goes on, but any changes must be gradual.

A breeder will also need to tell you what vaccinations the puppy has received; all details about the puppy's worming routine must also be made clear. Many breeders also provide temporary insurance for the puppy. In addition to health documents, the breeder should give you a copy of the pedigree registration papers, sales contract and guarantee, if he has one.

SELECTING A DACHSHUND BREEDER

Overview

- To find a reputable breeder do your research! Contact the American Kennel Club or the Dachshund Club of America.
- Know what to expect from a quality breeder. Ask questions, meet the dogs and pups and be prepared to wait for the most suitable pup.
- Good breeders come in large and small packages. Some large kennels are as reliable as small home breeders. Use strict critera for both.
- Ask about all relevant paperwork, which the breeder should provide upon purchase of your pup.

CHAPTER 5

Finding the Right Puppy

Observing the pups and their mother allows you to see how they interact and thus gain valuable insight into your prospective puppy's background.

You have located a dedicated breeder who has puppies available, so you are ready to take the next step—finding the perfect puppy for you. You should have the chance to visit the litter at around five or six weeks of age, but you will have to wait a few weeks longer before your puppy will be ready to come home with you.

A healthy puppy should be clean,

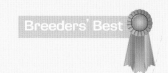

without any sign of discharge from the eyes or nose. His rear end should be spotless, with no sign of loose excreta. Although any puppy's nails can be sharp, the breeder should keep them trimmed.

The coat should be in excellent condition, and there should be no sign of parasites. Fleas and lice cannot always be seen easily, but will be indicated by the puppy's scratching, and you might notice a rash. Scratching, though, does not always mean that there is a skin condition, for it can also be associated with teething. In this case, the puppy will only scratch around his head area, and this will stop after the teething period. Scratching might also be connected to an ear infection, so a quick look inside the pup's ears will ensure that there is no build-up of wax, and there should be no odor from the ear. Of course, a good breeders will have checked that all

Handle with care! Dachshunds are small dogs and, as puppies, are tiny. Despite their diminutive size, they should not show fear of being handled and should be eager to meet you.

Your search is made a lot easier when your puppy picks you and the feeling is mutual!

pups are in good health!

Since all pure-bred dogs suffer from potential hereditary problems, responsible breeders screen their dogs before breeding. Check with the Dachshund Club of America to find out what health clearances are recommended, as Dachshunds are cited with many conditions that concern breeders. These include diabetes, epilepsy, disk disease, autoimmune thyroid disease and hypothyroidism and eye disease. A responsible breeder will have clearances from the Orthopedic Foundation for Animals (OFA) and the Canine Eye Registry Foundation (CERF) for both the sire and dam of the litter. You should ask to see written proof of the results.

Most puppies are outgoing and full of fun, so do not take pity on the overly shy one that hides away in a corner. Your puppy should clearly enjoy your company when you go along to visit. When you go to select your puppy, take with you the members of your immediate family with whom the puppy will spend time at home. It is essential that everyone agrees with the important decision you are about to make.

You should already have done plenty of research about the breed long before a new puppy enters your lives. The national parent club, the Dachshund Club of America, as well as regional breed clubs are important sources of help and information. Take advantage of these organizations. Some even publish their own leaflets and small booklets about the breed, and might even publish a book of champions, so that you can see what your puppy's famous ancestors looked like. There are also weekly and monthly canine newspapers or magazines that are available at newsstands or through subscriptions. These will give you a keen insight in who's who in the breeding and showing world, which could of interest to you if you are serious about acquiring a dog for competition.

Of course, you can find breed information on the Internet. However, I would urge you not to take all you read as the truth! Anyone can set up a website, even though he may not have sufficiently firm knowledge of the breed.

It is a good idea to become a member of at least one breed club. In doing so, you will meet other fanciers and receive notification of breed-specific events in which you may like to participate, thus providing further opportunities to learn about the Dachshund.

FINDING THE RIGHT PUPPY

Overview

- Visit the litter. Look for healthy, sound puppies with bright eyes, shiny coats and solid little frames.
- The breeder should be honest about discussing breed-specific health problems and showing you the parents' health clearance. Find out about OFA and CERF from the breeder and online.
- All family members should meet the litter and have a say in the puppy selection.
- If you intend to show, discuss this with the breeder. Purchase a dog magazine or newspaper to find out about dog shows and trials.
- Contact breeds clubs for information and consider becoming involved.

Welcoming the Dachshund

Now, whatever age you are, you can probably relive the excitement of a child's eagerly awaiting Christmas morn! Awaiting the arrival of a new puppy recaptures that same sort of excitement. In this case, though, you must be completely prepared, so that everything is ready and waiting for your new family member.

Sleeping quarters must be planned in advance. The pup's bed or crate should be very slightly raised so that there are no drafts, but not so high that your long, low puppy could injure himself by climbing in and out. Also, check your yard carefully so that there are no hidden escape routes, and

Children must be taught how to treat dogs and how to handle and carry them correctly. Hanging with his legs dangling is not good for any dog; one hand should be under the back legs for support.

make sure you have bought all of the items that your puppy is likely to need during his first few days with you.

You should have had the opportunity to meet and select your puppy before the day comes to bring him home. Should this be the case, you will have had plenty of chance to discuss with the breeder exactly what your puppy will need to make his life healthy, safe and enjoyable.

A Dachshund certainly can fit in a basket, but a safer mode of transport is his crate.

Depending on where you live, you will probably have easy access to a good pet-supply store, either one of the large outlets or a good privately owned shop. The major chains often have helpful, knowledgeable salespeople who know the merchandise well. If you can find an independent shop that is privately owned by people who show their own dogs, they often have a wide range of basic and specialty items, and will probably be able to give sensible guidance as to what you will need. Major dog shows

Are you ready for this small creature to become a huge part of your life?

You will need some grooming equipment for your Dachshund puppy. Basics are fine to start with, and you may need additional tools as your dog matures. This will vary according to your puppy's coat type, so take the breeder's advice about what equipment you should obtain. You will also need canine nail

also usually have many trade stands that cater to every dog-lover's need, and you are sure tobe absolutely spoiled for choice!

Select durable, easy-to-clean bowls, made of sturdy plastic or stainless steel, for your Dachshund.

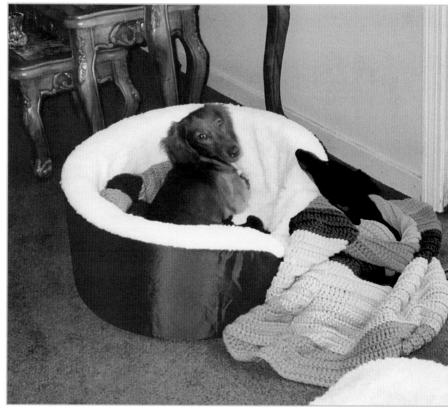

In addition to a crate as his own special place in the home, your Dachshund will enjoy a cozy bed in which he can curl up and rest.

clippers. You likely already have things like cotton swabs and towels in stock as household items.

Where your puppy is to sleep will be a major consideration, and you should start as you mean to go on. It is only natural that the newcomer will be restless for the first couple of nights or so, but if

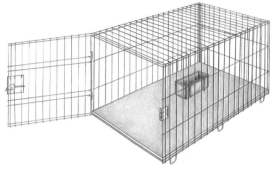

you immediately take pity on the little soul and let him join you in your bedroom, he will expect to remain there always! Hence, it is essential that the bedding you choose should be eminently suitable so that your puppy can rest as comfortably as possible in the intended place.

A wire crate is good for use indoors, as it provides the dog with a safe place of his own while allowing him to feel part of his surroundings, which will certainly be appreciated by your "nosy" Dachshund.

Assuming that your Dachshund puppy is to live in your home (as he should), rather than in a kennel, the choice of bedding is very much a matter of personal preference. Bearing in mind that a puppy will not want a bed that is too large, you may have to buy a small one to begin with and then a larger one a few months later.

Wicker beds may look

Dachshunds and their owners love to spend as much time together as possible, so a great benefit of your dog's size is that he can easily be taken with you most anywhere.

Buzz knows that the only way to travel is with his everyday collar and ID tags.

pretty, but they are dangerous because puppies chew them. Sharp wicker pieces can all too easily injure eyes or be swallowed to cause choking or internal injury. It is wiser to choose a durable bed that can be washed or wiped down, and easily lined with comfortable soft bedding that can be washed frequently. It is important that all of your dog's bedding is kept clean and dry (puppy "accidents" will happen!). Again, the bed should be just slightly raised from the ground or other-wised positioned to avoid drafts.

A Dachshund is small, so he can fit in all kinds of places and he can get into all kinds of mischief. Everyday household items may seem harmless enough, but a dainty cloth draped over the side of a table full of grandmother's china is merely asking for trouble! Even more dangerous to a mischievous puppy are electrical cables, so be sure

Equally as important as pupy-supply shopping is puppy-proofing your house. Dachshund pups are naturally curious critters that will investigate everything new, then seek-and-destroy just because it's fun. The message here is: Never let your puppy roam about your house unsupervised. Scout your house for the following hazards:

Trash Cans and Diaper Pails
These are natural puppy magnets (they know where the good smelly stuff is!).

Medication Bottles, Cleaning Materials, Roach and Rodent Poisons
Lock these up. You'll be amazed at what a determined puppy can find.

Electrical Cords
Unplug wherever you can and make the others inaccessible. Injuries from chewed electrical cords are extremely common in young dogs.

Dental Floss, Yarn, Needles and Thread, and Other Stringy Stuff
Puppies snuffling about at ground level will find and ingest the tiniest of objects and will end up in surgery. Most vets can tell you stories about the stuff they surgically removed from a puppy's gut.

Toilet-Bowl Cleaners
If you have them, throw them out now. All dogs are born with "toilet sonar" and quickly discover that the water there is always cold.

Garage Dangers
Beware of antifreeze! It is extremely toxic and even a few drops will kill an adult dog, even less for a pup. Lock it and all other chemicals well out of reach. Fertilizers can also be toxic to dogs.

Socks and Underwear, Shoes and Slippers, Too
Keep them off the floor and close your closet doors. Puppies love all of these items because they smell like *you times 10!*

Dachshund

Visit your pet shop and get a variety of safe toys. Your Dachshund will have fun playing with toys that encourage interaction between the two of you.

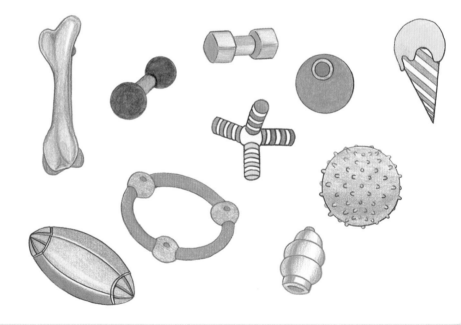

concerns cleaning agents, gardening aids and other household chemicals. Many of these contain substances that are poisonous, so please keep them out of the way of temptation.

The flexible lead extends to safely give your Dachshund a wider area to explore, and retracts when you need to keep your dog in close to you.

When your puppy first arrives home, it is only natural that you will be excited to show your new companion to your friends. However, your puppy is making a big move in his short life, so the first

they are concealed from his reach. Tiny teeth can bite through all too easily, causing what can be a fatal accident. Another word of warning

A lightweight yet sturdy nylon lead and collar will suffice for the adult Dachshund.

The most important thing you must have in your home is lots of love for your new family member.

two or three days are best spent quietly at home with you and your family. When your puppy has found his feet and taken stock of his new surroundings, you will be able to introduce him to lots of new people, provided he has received the necessary vaccinations. If you have young children, or if they visit, always carefully supervise any time spent with your young puppy. Youngsters can all too easily hurt a small puppy, even with the best of intentions.

If your family has other

Your new puppy depends on you for safety, guidance and affection.

pets, introductions should be made slowly and under close supervision. Most Dachshunds get along well with other animals if introduced sensibly, but you should always exercise caution until you are certain that all concerned are going to be the best of friends.

WELCOMING THE DACHSHUND

Overview

- Go on your puppy-supply shopping trip to have all necessities in place in advance of your pup's arrival home.
- Equally as important is to create a safe puppy-proof environment in your home, indoors and out. Be aware of most things around the house that could be doggie dangerous.
- Be prepared for some crying during your pup's first few nights. Choose his sleeping place wisely, provide him with a comfortable place to sleep and don't give into his whining. He will adjust in a short time.
- Once he's settled in, socializing the puppy will be fun for both of you.

Your Puppy's Education

When any puppy arrives at his new home, he will be unfamiliar with his surroundings and so initially will seem less extroverted than he was at the breeder's home. Do not be unduly concerned about this. Everything will be new to him and, when he has taken stock of his surroundings, your Dachshund will soon start to "feel his feet." He will look to you, his owner, to give him confidence in getting to know his strange new world.

Begin by getting him used to the members of your family who live in

Don't overwhelm your Dachshund with too many introductions all at once. Take each one slowly, and your Dachshund will have a new circle of friends before you know it.

the home. Soon you will be able to introduce him to your larger circle of family and friends. Please try not to bombard him with too many new people and situations, all at the same time, as this would overwhelm him.

Depending on the age of your puppy, and whether his course of vaccinations is complete, you may or may not be able to take him out in public places immediately. Whichever the case, I would still advise you to allow him to settle down at home for the first few days before venturing further. There will be lots you can do at home with your Dachshund puppy, so you will both undoubtedly have great fun, but please allow him to get sufficient rest, too.

If restricted to your home for a little while, you can play games together with suitably safe, soft toys. Never allow him to tug on anything too strongly. Check regularly that poten-tially unsafe parts, such as "squeaks,"

Children and Dachshunds get along wonderfully, provided that the relationship is based on careful handling and respectful treatment of the dog.

Well-socialized Dachshunds love to snuggle up with their canine pals. Here are happy housemates Astrid and Steffi sharing a some downtime.

do not become detached from any toy. These small parts can cause injury, and your puppy's teeth will be very sharp and thus easily able to damage soft toys.

During your first few days at home, you also can get started with a little early training. Introduce your pup to standing calmly on a table and being gently groomed. This will be helpful on numerous occasions, including your routine grooming sessions and visits to the vet, when it is much easier to deal with a well-behaved dog. You will be so proud of your clever companion!

Accustom your puppy to being on a lead, which is always a strange experience for a tiny youngster. Begin by just attaching a simple collar, not too tightly, but not so loose that it can be caught on things, causing panic and possible injury. Just put it on for a few minutes at a time, lengthening each time period slightly until your puppy feels comfortable

Your puppy spent at least the first eight weeks of his life as part of a pack, and the companion-ship of his littermates is what he will miss most when he first comes home.

Engage your Dachshund in games with her toys. Astrid is an avid retriever, just waiting for someone to throw her ball!

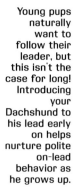

Young pups naturally want to follow their leader, but this isn't the case for long! Introducing your Dachshund to his lead early on helps nurture polite on-lead behavior as he grows up.

in his first item of "clothing." Don't expect miracles; this may take a few days.

Then, when he is comfortable in the collar, attach a small, lightweight lead. The one you select must have a secure catch, yet be simple to attach and release as necessary. Until now, your puppy has simply gone where he has pleased, and will find it very strange to be attached to someone who is restricting his movements. For this reason,

when training my own puppies, I like to allow them to "take" me for the first few sessions, then I start to exert a little pressure. Soon enough, training can start in earnest, with the puppy coming with me as I lead the way.

It is usual to begin training the puppy to walk on your left-hand side. When this has been accomplished to your satisfaction, you can try moving him on your right but there is absolutely no hurry. If you plan to show your Dachshund, you will generally move your dog on your left, but there are occasions when it is necessary also to move him on your right so as not to obstruct the judge's view.

As your puppy gets older you can teach him to sit, always using a simple one-word of command, "Sit," while exerting gentle pressure on his rump to guide him into the position that you expect. This will take a little time, but you

Whether working with a puppy or adult, keep initial training sessions short and fun.

Hot dog! This whimsical lead, surely designed just with the Dachshund in mind, was purchased in Denmark, showing that Dachshund lovers the world over share a sense of humor about their favorite breed.

A wire "ex-pen," like the one shown here, is useful for giving your Dachshund a place of safe confinement outdoors, whether in your own yard or when traveling.

will soon succeed. Always giving plenty of praise when appropriate!

Never shout or get angry when your dog does not will find his confidence increasing, and you can then introduce him to new dog-friendly places with exciting sights, sounds and smells. He

Consider your Dachshund's tiny size combined with his curiosity and you'll see why supervision is necessary.

achieve your aim, for this will do more harm than good. If yours is destined to be a show dog, you may decide not to teach "sit," as in the show ring he will be expected to stand. Nonetheless, good manners are required.

When your Dachshund puppy can venture into public places, begin by taking him somewhere quiet without too many distractions. Soon you must always be on a safe lead that cannot be slipped. When you have total confidence in one another, you may be able to let him off-lead, but always keep him in sight. Be absolutely sure that the place you have chosen for free exercise is utterly safe and securely enclosed, and that no strange dogs can suddenly appear from "nowhere"!

Whether you have a show

Make sure your puppy is comfortable with all of the family members and give him time to settle into his new home before any type of training (except house-training!) begins.

dog or a pet, you will need to train your puppy to stay in a crate when required. At shows in most countries, smaller breeds are housed in crates for at least part of the time while not being actually exhibited in the ring. Crates are useful for traveling, and if used in the home, most dogs seem to look upon them as safe places to go and don't mind staying in for short periods. This can be helpful sometimes if you are out of the house or otherwise cannot supervise your dog.

The crate is also an essential component of house-training. When you commence crate training, remain within sight of your dog and give him a toy or treat to occupy him.

To begin, leave him in the crate for very short spells of just a minute or two, then gradually build up the timespan. However, never confine a dog to a crate for long periods, for this would be unkind.

YOUR PUPPY'S EDUCATION

Overview

- Spend time with your new puppy, helping him become comfortable in his new home and laying a solid foundation for your dog lover bond. Play games with safe toys.
- Introduce him to the outside world a little at a time—don't cause him sensory overload!
- Wearing his collar, walking on his lead and standing on the grooming table are basic lessons you can teach before progressing to the basic commands.
- Positive reinforcement is the way to go. Always let your puppy know when he's behaving correctly.
- Introduce the puppy to his crate in short, gradually increasing, periods of time.

House-training the Dachshund

The first training endeavor you'll begin with your Dachshund puppy is house-training, and that should begin right away when your puppy comes home.

When training any young, intelligent, alert dog, patience is a virtue! Your Dachshund will probably look up at you with that characteristic defiant carriage of the head and those captivating eyes, and you will wonder what he will decide to do next. To obey or not to obey? That is the question. Your pup is certainly capable of being trained, but, if he is to understand what is required of him, you will need to be sensible and consistent in all training. To house-train successfully, you will need to be firm, but never harsh. Use a happy voice for giving praise and a serious tone when giving reprimands.

When your puppy first arrives at your home, he may or may not already have begun his house-training, likely only to a limited extent. However, you must realize that your home is completely different from the breeder's, so the pup will have to relearn the house rules. Doors will not be located in the same places and your family may go to bed and rise at different times, so it will undoubtedly take him a little time to adapt.

The speed of your house-training success will depend to a certain extent on your living environment and on the season of the year. Most puppies are perfectly happy to go out into the backyard in dry weather, but when the rain is pouring down, many will need considerable encouragement! Likewise, some dogs (especially smooths) disdain the winter months and may be reluctant to "rough" the frigid morning air.

Once house-trained, your Dachshund will have no trouble following his nose to locate his relief site and returning there to use it each time he takes a potty break.

Your Dachshund puppy is just a "baby" in the dog world, without the benefit of a diaper! The sooner you start house-training, the sooner you'll have a dog with good toileting habits.

CRATE TRAINING

The crate is a natural house-training aid. Your Dachshund puppy is an inherently clean little fellow and he will try hard not to soil his "den" or living space. Thus, his crate is actually a multi-purpose dog accessory: your Dachshund's personal home within your home, a humane house-training tool, a security measure that will protect your household and furniture when you cannot supervise, a travel aid to house and protect your dog when you are traveling (most motels will accept a crated dog) and, finally, a comfy dog space for your Dachshund when your anti-dog relatives come to visit.

Introduce the crate as soon as he comes home so that he learns that this is his new "house." This is best accomplished with treats! For the first day or two, toss a tiny treat into the crate to entice the pup to go in. Pick a crate command, such as "Inside" or "Crate," and use it every time he enters. You also can feed his first few meals inside the crate with the door still open, so the crate association will be a happy one.

You must keep a careful eye on your puppy. Routines, consistency and an eagle eye are your keys to house-training success. Puppies always "go" when they wake up, within a few minutes after eating, after play periods, and after brief periods of confinement. Your pup should sleep in his crate, so don't put a bowl of water in there with him. This is asking for puddles. At night, remove the puppy's water after 7 p.m. to aid in nighttime bladder control. If he gets thirsty, offer him an ice cube. Then just watch him race for the refrigerator when he hears the rattle of the ice-cube tray!

Although it may seem like a good idea to use the crate to "send the puppy to his room," *never* use the crate for punishment. Successful crate use depends on your puppy's positive association with his "house." If the crate represents punishment or "bad-dog stuff," he will resist using it as his safe

crate by overuse. Puppies under 12 weeks of age should never be confined for more than two hours at a time unless, of course, they are

Experienced breeders introduce their puppies to crates early on. This proves advantageous to new owners lucky enough to adopt such pups.

place. Sure, you can crate your pup after he has sorted through the trash. Just don't do it in an angry fashion or tell him "Bad dog, crate!"

Further, do not abuse the

sleeping. A general rule of thumb is three hours maximum for a three-month old pup, four to five hours for the four- or five-month-old and no more than six hours for dogs over six months of age. If you're unable to be home to release the dog, arrange for a relative, neighbor or dog-sitter to let him out to exercise and potty.

**A CLEAN LIFE
WITH YOUR DACHSHUND**

Paper training can be useful in the very early stages of training. Paper should be placed by the door so that the dog learns to associate the paper with the exit to the wide world outside. When he uses the paper, he should be praised. Obviously, it is ideal if the puppy can be let outside as

If you don't want your Dachshund to use the flower garden as his toilet, don't allow him to go there. Pick a remote area of the yard and don't forget the pooper scooper!

soon as he shows any sign of wanting to do his business, but again this may depend on whether your home has immediate access to a yard or you, at least, don't live on the 23rd floor.

Remember that puppies need to go out much more frequently than adult dogs, certainly immediately after waking and following meals. In fact, to take your pup outside every hour while he is awake is not a bad idea at all. Always keep your eyes and ears open, for a youngster will not be able to wait those extra two or three minutes until it is convenient for you to let him out. If you delay, accidents will certainly happen, so be warned!

As your puppy matures, his "asking" to be let out when necessary will become second nature. It is rare that you will have a Dachshund that is unclean in the house. A stud dog, however, can be different, for he may well want to mark his territory, and your table and chair legs may be just the places he chooses!

Simple one-word commands are very helpful, "Potty" being my own favorite, and it seems to work. Never, ever forget to give praise when the deed is done in the desired place. However, if an accident happens your puppy should be given a verbal reprimand, but this will only work if your Dachshund is caught in the act. If you try to reprimand him after the fact, he will simply not know what he has done wrong, which will only serve to confuse him.

It is essential that any messes are cleaned up immediately. If a dog has done his business in the wrong place, it must be cleaned thoroughly so as to disguise the smell or else he will want to use that particular place again. When your puppy is old enough to be exercised in public places, always carry with you a pooper scooper or small plastic bag so that any droppings can be removed. The anti-dog lobby exists everywhere, so please give them no cause for complaint.

HOUSE-TRAINING THE DACHSHUND

Overview

- The first step for all puppy owners is housebreaking, teaching the dog proper toileting habits.
- The crate is the best tool to help your house-training efforts. If used correctly, the crate offers many advantages to dog owners.
- Pick a relief command and use it each time you take your puppy out to relieve himself.
- Know the times at which your pup will need to go out, and don't ignore the signs he gives you.
- You might start out with paper-training and then progress to teaching the pup to relieve himself outdoors.

Teaching Basic Commands

Teaching a dog to respond to basic commands is not only necessary but also highly rewarding. Because the Dachshund is an intelligent little dog, he can be a willing learner. However, you must always be consistent in your approach and remember that this is a fun-loving breed that may not always respond as you expect. Some trainers may redefine "fun-loving" in this context to mean "stubborn" or "thick-headed." However you look at it, Dachshunds do take a little more firmness and patience than some other breeds.

Training your Dachshund means more than just commands. It also means teaching your dog the rules of the house and what behaviors you will and will not accept.

Keep in mind, too, that the Dachshund is a bright hound dog. Hounds do not accept instruction as readily as, say, a Golden Retriever or German Shepherd. Further, because of the Dachshund's length of body, he cannot be expected to sit quite as neatly when doing obedience work as would a Border Collie. This you will simply have to accept, for your Dachshund is just made that way!

Use a training method based on positive reinforcement, using food rewards and praise to let your Dachshund know when he's done the right thing.

Although some show dogs are trained in obedience, many exhibitors feel this can be detrimental to a dog's performance in the show ring. Nonetheless, all dogs must be taught basic good manners, but which commands you choose to teach may differ if you aspire to show.

In all training, it is essential to get your dog's full attention, which many owners do with the aid of treats so that the dog learns to associate treats with praise and thus praise with good things.

Something *really* interesting must be going on to distract Sparkle, a field-trial champion, from the treat that's only inches away!

The following training method involves using food treats, although you will eventually wean your dog off food rewards as your training progresses until you are left with a primarily praise-based reward system. Always use very simple commands; short one-word commands are the most effective. Keep training sessions short, so that they do not become too repetitive and thus boring for your dog.

SIT COMMAND

With the lead in your left hand and hold a small treat in your right, letting your dog smell or lick the treat, but not take it. Move it away as you say "Sit," your hand rising slowly over the dog's head so that he looks upward. In doing so he will bend his knees, and will sit. When this has been accomplished, give him the treat and lavish praise.

The first few times that you attempt the sit exercise, you may need to gently guide your Dachshund into the correct position so that he knows what is expected of him.

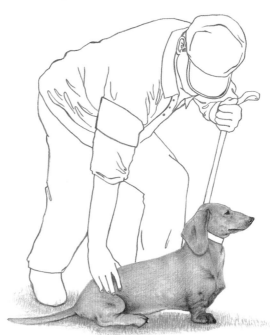

The heel exercise is not just for show dogs. Your daily walks will be a struggle, rather than a pleasure, if you have a dog that's constantly pulling and tugging on the lead.

HEEL COMMAND

A dog trained to walk to heel will walk alongside his handler without pulling. Again the lead should be held in your left hand, while the dog assumes the sit position next to your left leg. Hold the end of the lead in your right hand, but also control it lower down with your left.

Step forward with your right foot, saying "Heel." To begin, just take three steps, then command him to sit again. Repeat this procedure until he carries out the task without pulling. You can then increase the number of strides to five, seven and so on. Give verbal praise at the close of each section of the exercise and, at the end of the training session, let him enjoy himself with some free play.

CHAPTER 9

DOWN COMMAND

When your dog is proficient in sitting, you can introduce the down command. You must first understand that a dog will consider the down position as a submissive one, so gentle training is extra-important.

With your Dachshund sitting by your left leg, as for the sit, hold the lead in your left hand and a treat in your right. Place your left hand gently on top of the dog's shoulders (without pushing) and hold the treat under his nose, saying "Down," in a quiet tone of voice. Gradually move the treat along the floor, in front of the dog, all the while talking gently. He will follow the food, lowering himself down. When his elbows touch the floor, you can release the treat and give praise, but try to get him to remain in position for a few seconds before getting up. Gradually the time of the down exercise can be increased.

STAY COMMAND

Stay can be taught with your dog in either a sit or down position, as usual with he lead in your left hand and the treat in your right. Allow him to lick the treat as you say "Stay," while standing directly in front of the dog, having moved from your position beside him. Silently count to about five, then move back to your original position alongside him, allowing your dog to have the treat while giving him praise.

Keep practicing the stay

The Dachshund doesn't have very far to go to reach the down position; nonetheless, this exercise is difficult for all dogs as it indicates a submissive posture.

just as described for a few days, then gradually increase the distance between you. Use your hand with the palm facing the dog as a "stop" sign, indicating that he must stay. Soon you should be able to do this exercise without a lead, and your Dachshund will stay for increasingly longer periods of time. Always give lavish praise upon completion of the exercise. Only attempt exercises off-lead in a securely enclosed area.

COME COMMAND

Your Dachshund will learn to love to come back to you when called. The idea is to invite him to

return, offering a treat and giving lots of praise when he does so. It is important to teach the come command, for this should bring your dog running back to you if ever he is danger of moving out of sight.

Teaching your dog to stay in the sit or down position is a natural follow-up to the sit and down exercises. Use hand signals along with your verbal command to get your message across.

Field training is more involved, but has its foundation in the basic commands. Here the dog stays sitting by the hunter's side until commanded to do otherwise.

You cannot risk failure with the come command, as it is essential for his safety that he reliably returns to you every time you call him. Thus, you must never call your dog to discipline or scold him. He must always connect coming to you with praise, treats, petting or other positive things—positive reinforcement.

You always want your Dachshund to respond eagerly when you call him to come to you.

TRICKS

The Dachshund is a remarkable little character that may well enjoy learning a trick or two. What trick you teach, if anything at all, will be a matter of choice. Again, you will have to consider that the Dachshund's bodily construction is rather different from that of other breeds! Simple tricks like sitting up and begging are difficult but not impossible. Start with rolling over as this is every Dachshund's easiest stunt.

Your training will progress to the next level if you choose to show your dog. Aside from heeling, show dogs are expected to stay in the standing position for extended periods of time in the ring.

TEACHING BASIC COMMANDS

Overview

- Consider your Dachshund's sometimes clownish, sometimes stubborn personality when planning your lesson.
- Training begins by getting and maintaining your puppy's attention.
- The best training method is based on positive reinforcement, using rewards of food and praise.
- Keep lessons short and upbeat, allowing play in between, to prevent your Dachshund from becoming bored.
- The basic commands include come, sit, stay, down and heel.
- Practice with your Dachshund daily so that he's 100% consistent.

Home Care for Your Dachshund

A healthy Dachshund generally lives somewhere between 10 and 16 years. Remember that a Dachshund thrives best with plenty of outdoor exercise. One that is constantly confined to the sofa, resulting in soft condition and excess weight, cannot be expected to live as long.

Because you will grow to understand your Dachshund well, you will learn to recognize any signs that he is not feeling his usual sprightly self. This will help you to see problems arising, so that you can

Brushing your dog's teeth is part of your responsibility. Your vet can show you how to do it properly and what products to use.

...ake your pet to the vet without delay 'or further examination. With all medical problems, the earlier they are ...reated, the better.

DENTAL CARE

...eeping teeth in good condition is your responsibility, and you owe this ...o your dog. Dental problems do not ...ust stop inside the mouth. When ...gums are infected, all sorts of health problems can subsequently arise as ...he infection can spread through the ...dog's system, affecting the vital organs and possibly leading even to ...death.

Your Dachshund should have a comfortable place to sleep, situated in a spot away from drafts.

You may clean your Dachshund's ...eeth using a small toothbrush and ...special canine toothpaste. Take ...particular care if any of the teeth are ...beginning to loosen. Your dog may ...not like this procedure much at first, ...but should easily get used to it if you ...clean regularly. Experienced breeders ...sometimes use a special dental

Although he looks just as sweet, your Dachshund is not a stuffed toy but a living animal that needs your love and care.

scraper, but this is not recommended for use by the average pet owner as damage can be done if used incorrectly.

A relatively new product on the market is a special dental paste that is smeared onto the teeth regularly, without the use of a toothbrush. This is effective in breaking down any tartar that may have built up.

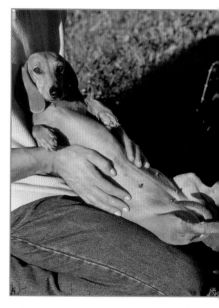

Tattooing is one permanent form of identification. The light skin on the belly is often chosen for the tattoo, as it makes the ID number easy to read.

When cleaning the teeth, always check the gums for signs of inflammation. If you notice that the gums look red or swollen, a visit to your vet is advised.

FIRST AID

Accidents can happen. If they do, you must remain as cool, calm and collected as possible under the circumstances so that you can give your dog the help he needs while contacting the vet.

Insect stings are quite common. If your dog is stung and the "stinger" is left in him, it should be removed with tweezers. Ice can be applied to reduce the swelling and accurate dosage of antihistamine treatment given. If a sting is inside the mouth, consult your vet at once.

Accidental poisoning is also a worry, as dogs can investigate all sorts of things, not all of which are safe. If you suspect poisoning, try to ascertain the cause, because treatment may vary according to the type of poison injested. Vomiting or sudden bleeding from an exit point, such as the gums, can indicate poisoning. Urgent veterinary attention is essential.

Small abrasions should be cleaned thoroughly and antiseptic applied. In the case of serious bleeding, initially apply pressure above the area. For minor burns, apply cool water. In the case of shock, such as following a car accident, keep the dog warm while veterinary aid is sought without delay.

For heat stroke, cold water must be applied immediately, especially over the shoulders. In severe cases, if possible, the dog should be submerged in water up to his neck. Dogs can die quickly from heat stroke, so urgent veterinary attention is of paramount importance. Conversely, in the case of hypothermia, keep the dog warm with hot-water bottles and give a warm bath if possible while waiting veterinary attention.

RECOGNIZING HEALTH SIGNS

If you love your Dachshund and you spend plenty of time together, you will get to know him well and thus will recognize when something is amiss. He may go off his food or seem dull and listless. His

Traveling in style! Whether it's a ride around the block, a visit to the vet or a longer road trip, you must consider your Dachshund's comfort and safety while traveling. Owner, Carla Aldarelli.

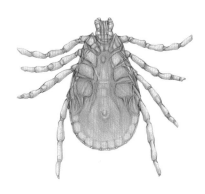

With eight strong legs, a tick can easily latch on to a dog and hold on for dear life, as he thrives by feeding on your dog's blood.

eyes, usually bright and alive, may seem to have lost their sparkle and his coat may look dull.

Your dog's excretions may also be an indication of ill health. Loose motions usually clear up within 24 hours but, if they go on for longer than this, especially if you see blood, you will need to visit your vet. Also keep a look out for increased thirst and an increase in frequency of

urination, which could be indicative of any of various problems.

CHECKING FOR PARASITES

It is essential to keep your dog's coat in first-rate order or else parasites may take a hold, causing skin and coat condition to deteriorate. It is often not easy to see parasites and, be assured, if you catch sight of even one flea, you can be sure there will be more lurking somewhere! There are now several good preventative aids available for external parasites, and your vet will advise you about which are the most effective. Sometimes the best remedies are not available in pet shops.

Also be on the continual look out for ear mites. These cannot be seen, but a brown discharge with foul odor in the ear is a clear indication that ear mites are present. A suitable ear treatment will be available from your vet.

A magnified look at a flea gives you an idea of just how scary these pests can be!

A dog can also carry internal parasites in the form of worms. Roundworms are the most common. Tapeworms, although less frequent, can be even more debilitating. Heartworms are transmitted by mosquitoes, though this disease is not as common as you might think. If you live in a heavily forested area in which mosquitoes are everyday bothers, then by all means give your Dachshund one of the heartworm preventatives prescribed at the vet's office. Since these remedies introduce poisons into your dog's system, consider them carefully before putting your dog on a preventative regimen. Discuss with your vet the necessity of protecting your Dachshund and the safest way to do so. Routine worming is essential throughout a dog's life and, again, veterinary recommendation as to the safest regimen is necessary.

HOME CARE FOR YOUR DACHSHUND

Overview

- Dental care should be foremost on every Dachshund owner's home-care routine. Brush your Dachshund's teeth to promote clean teeth and fresh-smelling breath.
- First aid should never be a second thought. Be prepared for common problems like bee stings, poison ingestion and heat stroke.
- During weekly grooming sessions, keep an eye on the condition of your Dachshund's coat. Always watch for moles, bumps, lumps and parasites, all of which can lead to serious problems.
- Know the signs of wellness so that you can recognize when your Dachshund's health may be compromised by disease.

Feeding Your Dachshund

Dachshunds tend to really enjoy their food, so you will have to take great care that you do not allow yours to put on excess weight. Extra weight puts additional strain on the heart and on the joints, and puts a dog under increased risk when under anesthesia. Today there is an enormous range of specially prepared foods available for dogs, many of them scientifically balanced and suitable for specific age ranges. It is really a matter of personal preference as to which food you

A safe sturdy chew is a good "dessert," as it helps to scrape away any plaque or tartar.

choose, as long as it provides complete and balanced nutrition. Initially your choice will be influenced by the type of food that has been fed to your new puppy by his breeder. Changes can be made to the pup's diet, but never change suddenly from one food to another, or your Dachshund is likely to get an upset belly. Introduce a new brand of food gradually, over a few days, until the old brand is phased out. There is usually no harm at all in changing the flavor of food, while keeping with the same brand, to add a bit of variety. You might prefer to add a little flavored stock to tempt the palate. Regardless, be aware that too many changes can lead to finicky habits.

Your Dachshund should be fed in the same spot for each meal, in a low-traffic area where he can eat in peace.

Should you decide to feed a dry food, be sure to thoroughly read the feeding instructions. For all Dachshunds, but especially for Miniatures, you should choose a dry food

Don't share your dinner with your Dachshund! Feeding "people" food to your dog has many disadvantages, including upset stomach, weight gain and encouraging begging or finicky eating.

described as "small bite" size. Some dry foods need to be soaked, especially those for youngsters. Dry foods should be stored carefully, bearing in mind that its vitamin value declines if not used fairly quickly, usually within about three months. It is essential that a plentiful supply of fresh water is available for your dog when feeding dry foods in particular, though dogs should, of course, have access to water at all times.

Because of the enormous range of products available, you may find it difficult to make a choice without advice from your vet, breeder or another Dachshund enthusiast. Here are a few general tips: Keep in mind that, in adulthood, an active dog will

Treats are welcomed by all dogs and are useful in training, but don't overdo it. A small dog like the Dachshund can easily put on ounces (or pounds!) if given too many extras.

Quality food has a bearing on your Dachshund's overall condition, including proper weight, coat, activity level and general health.

require a higher protein content than one that leads a sedentary life. Also, no dog should be fed chocolate, as this is carcinogenic to dogs. Onions, raisins, grapes and nuts are among some other "people foods" toxic to dogs.

Some owners prefer to feed fresh foods, but, in this case, owners must be absolutely certain that they are feeding well-balanced diets. There currently seems to be a move toward reverting back to the more natural diet of the wild, and some owners even give raw chicken wings, which dogs seem to thoroughly enjoy. Many say this helps to keep teeth clean and breath fresh. Cooked vegetables are also beneficial to this type of diet. Again, owners must be thoroughly educated in how to properly and safely offer this type of diet.

Many owners are tempted to feed tidbits between meals, but, aside from your judicious use of treats in training, this is not a good idea. Too many treats can cause weight to pile on almost imperceptibly! A suitable treat is an occasional

Pups get the best start in their lives from nursing from their mother, as the mother's milk contains colostrum that gives the pups both nutrition and resistance to disease.

piece of carrot. Most dogs love them! Carrots don't put on any weight and are another useful aid in keeping the teeth clean.

How many times a day you feed your adult Dachshund will probably be a matter of personal preference and your daily routine. Many feed two meals daily once in the morning and once in the evening, rather than one large meal. Obviously, puppies need to be fed more frequently than adults, but your breeder will have given you good advice in this regard, and the transition to the adult schedule will be made gradually.

As a dog gets older, his metabolism changes, so feeding requirements may change, too. This can mean feeding smaller, more easily digestible portions, more frequently throughout the day. By then, of course, you will know your pet well and should be able to adjust feeding accordingly. If you have any queries, your vet will be able to guide you in the right direction.

FEEDING YOUR DACHSHUND

Overview

- Balanced and complete nutrition is what counts when feeding any dog. A top-quality dog food is the most reliable and convenient way to provide this to your Dachshund.
- Discuss with your vet and/or breeder amounts, types of food and feeding schedule for your Dachshund at all stages of life.
- Don't let your Dachshund become a "chow hound." Obesity predisposes dogs to many health problems, and the food-loving Dachshund can be prone to putting on the weight.
- Your attention to your Dachshund's diet largely affects his overall health and condition.

Grooming Your Dachshund

Because the Dachshund is seen in three different coat types, this is a subject about which a puppy buyer must take expert advice from the breeder, depending on the coat type of the individual puppy. Clearly, grooming a smooth Dachshund takes considerably less time than it does for a longhaired or a wirehaired variety, but all three coat types need regular coat attention. Coat care is an essential part of canine maintenance,

Examine your dog's mouth and teeth often and make toothbrushing part of his grooming sessions, daily if possible.

and the grooming procedure can be pleasurable for both dog and owner. Grooming will almost undoubtedly strengthen the bond between you and your dog.

Ideally, your Dachshund will be groomed on a firm table with a non-slip surface. A grooming table from a pet-supply shop will be a worthwhile investment, especially if you have a wirehair or longhair. You will find that Dachshund owners use different pieces of equipment according to what they find suits best and, of course, according to coat type. You will get good advice from your breeder about this when you bring home your new puppy and, as you gain experience, you will develop your own preferences.

Love and reassurance during puppy pedicures will help your Dachshund become accustomed to having his nails clipped.

COAT CARE

It is essential to keep your Dachshund's coat clean and to groom him regularly. How frequently you bathe your dog will depend on his coat type and

Clean your Dachshund's ears regularly and gently with a soft wipe and ear-cleaning powder or liquid, available from your local pet shop.

whether or not yours is a show dog. Exhibitors have individual preferences as to how long before a show they bathe their dogs, or whether they bathe at all. In the case of wirehairs, bathing softens the coat, so generally bathing is not advised.

SMOOTHS

Brushing the smooth coat every day serves to stimulate the coat and to rid it of any dead hair. Nose, eyes, anal area and genital area should be wiped gently with warm water on a cotton ball or similar pad to keep them clean, and to prevent any buildup of fecal matter.

Some smooths get dandruff, in which case it is wise to add a little extra oil to the diet for a few days; ask the vet about this and any dietary changes for coat condition. Massaging baby oil or almond oil into the coat prior to bathing can also help. An ideal coat has a waxy shine to it, with the hair lying flat to the body. That is what you should aim for. Some owners like to

The smooth coat is the easiest to maintain. A hound glove or grooming mitt is a good tool to go over the smooth, removing dead hair and imparting a rich sheen.

The long coat requires extra attention to the long feathering, ensuring that no mats and tangles occur and also that the dog's long coat does not pick up debris from the ground.

use a chamois leather or piece of velvet for the finishing touch.

LONGHAIRS

Perhaps surprisingly, among the longhaired variety of Dachshund there are various different types of coat, and each has to be dealt with in the best way for that particular dog. It is essential for a new owner to take advice from those with experience in the breed.

In general, longhairs need bathing more frequently than smooths, but still it will be for the owner to decide how often to bathe to retain the best-quality coat. Longs certainly need brushing daily with a soft wire brush, which will remove any mats or tangles that may have imperceptibly built up. Any soiled areas of the coat should also be washed and dried.

There is little trimming on a longhaired Dachshund, just

on the feet. Hair growing between the pads of the feet should be carefully trimmed away and the tops of the toes and instep should be tidied up. Any long hair that looks unsightly can usually be plucked carefully with your thumb and forefinger.

WIREHAIRS

The most demanding of the three coat types is the wire-haired variety. This coat type requires daily grooming and, although not usually bathed, the coat will need to be stripped. Stripping is a method of plucking the coat to maintain proper texture. The easiest type of wirehaired coat is what is known as a "pin-wire," as this needs much less attention, but such coats are few and far between.

Stripping a show dog's coat is usually done with the thumb and forefinger, but pets are often stripped using a stripping knife and scissors. The only way to learn how to strip properly is to watch those who have had much practice.

The wire coat is maintained much like that of a terrier, involving hand stripping to keep the desired harsh texture.

Owners of wirehaired Dachshunds are usually very generous with their advice. As a new owner, you will learn much more from seeing the grooming process in action than you will from reading a book. As with longs, it is necessary to remove hair from between the pads of the wirehair's feet.

EARS AND EYES

It is important to keep your Dachshund's eyes and ears clean. They should be carefully wiped, perhaps using one of the proprietary cleaners available from good pet stores.

If your dog has been shaking his head or scratching at his ears, there may well be an infection or ear mites. Likewise, your dog may be carrying his head in a tilted fashion, which also indicates a problem. A thick brown discharge and malodorous smell are also indicative of these problems, so veterinary consultation is needed right away.

At any sign of injury to the eye, or if the eye turns blue, veterinary help must be sought immediately. If an eye injury is dealt with quickly, it can often be repaired; if neglected, it can lead to loss of sight.

NAILS AND FEET

Nails must always be kept at a proper length. How frequently they need clipping depends very much on the surface upon which your dog walks. Dogs living their lives primarily on carpets or on grass will need more frequent attention to their nails than those who regularly walk on hard surfaces.

What's hiding in your Dachshund's coat? Although longhairs are most susceptible to picking up "passengers," the skin and coats of Dachshunds of all varieties should be checked after time spent outdoors.

Your Dachshund should be trained to accept nail clipping from an early age. Take great care not to cut into the quick, which is the blood vessel that runs through the nail, for this

Dachshund

Walking on hard surfaces will keep your Dachshund's nails at a good length naturally. Nonetheless, he should be introduced to nail clippers at an early age, as he inevitably will need trims from time to time.

will be painful for the dog. It is a good idea to keep a styptic pencil or styptic powder on hand to stem the flow of blood in case of an accident. Cutting just a small slither of nail at a time is the safest approach. You should also inspect the feet regularly to be sure that nothing has become wedged or embedded between the pads.

ANAL GLANDS

A dog's anal glands are located on either side of the anal opening. Sometimes these become blocked and require evacuation, signaled by the dog's squatting and trying to rub his rear end on the ground or carpet. Experienced breeders often express the glands themselves, but pet owners would be well advised to leave this to their vet. Not only can an inexperienced owner cause damage, but expressing the glands is a rather unpleasant task. Sometimes, surgical evacuation is necessary. Firm stools help to evacuate the anal glands naturally, so diet will have a bearing on this.

GROOMING YOUR DACHSHUND

Overview

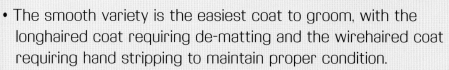

- The smooth variety is the easiest coat to groom, with the longhaired coat requiring de-matting and the wirehaired coat requiring hand stripping to maintain proper condition.
- Frequency of bathing depends on coat type and whether your Dachshund is shown, but too-frequent bathing is not recommended.
- Your breeder or another fancier with experience in your dog's coat type will be an invaluable source of grooming advice.
- Along with your dog's coat, you must tend to his nails, eyes, ears and anal sacs for overall health and cleanliness.

DACHSHUND

Keeping the Dachshund Active

Every dog loves to investigate new places and new smells, and this certainly holds true for the Dachshund. Regular activity not only will help to keep him fit but also will serve to keep his senses alert. Although small, your Dachshund should be kept in the peak of physical condition. He was never meant to be a "lapdog." However, please be aware that many Dachshunds seem to have little road sense, so they should always be kept on a short lead near traffic.

When out for walks, you must keep foremost in your mind that this is a

For earthdog events, in which Dachshunds compete along with the terriers, dogs have traditionally worn bells around their necks to help their handlers locate them when the dogs are underground.

small breed, long and low to the ground, so accidents could happen. For example, larger heavier dogs can be encountered. Also remember that the Dachshund is a hound, with a great hunting instinct. Therefore, "on-lead only" is a good rule of thumb when out in public to avoid your Dachshund's taking off in hot pursuit of some perceived "prey."

Nosy Dachshunds keep themselves busy by using their acute sense of smell to follow whatever odor strikes their fancy. Exploring is even more fun with a partner!

Unless your Dachshund has been brought up with children, he might take exception to toddlers approaching him unexpectedly. Being something of a barker, he might well decide to "retaliate" with noise, which could frighten the child and probably make matters worse, so keep your wits about you when out walking! It is also important that your Dachshund is not left damp following exercise in inclement weather.

Some Dachshunds are used in therapy work, visiting nursing homes and hospitals to meet the people there

Elsa von Dampfnudl is a pampered lady about town, traveling in style by limo.

Dachshund

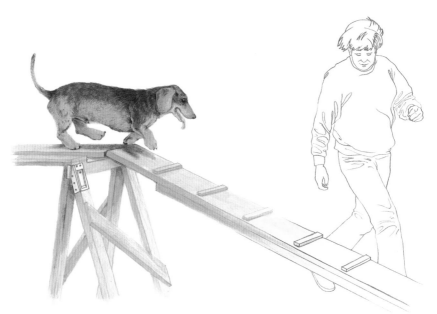

Up and over the agility A-frame. The obstacles in agility trials for small dogs are adjusted to compensate for smaller stature, meaning that all dogs can try their "paw" at agility and have a chance at success, no matter their size.

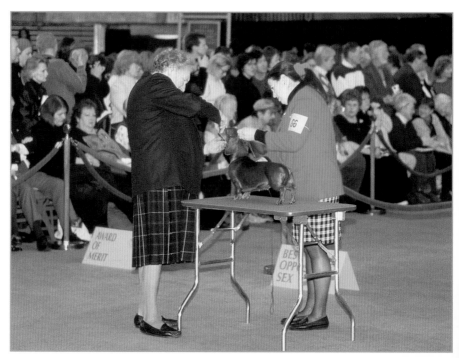

Conformation showing is popular among Dachshund fanciers and can be very entertaining for fanciers, allowing them to see all coat types and size varieties.

and brighten their days with some cuddles and companionship. The breed's convenient size and charming personality make these visits something to which hospital patients and the elderly greatly look forward. It is also possible for a Dachshund to become a "hearing dog." This is a dog that is especially trained to listen for sounds like telephones and doorbells ringing, which is of great assistance to an owner with impaired hearing.

Dachshunds take part in dog shows, competitive obedience trials, agility trials and earthdog events. Even if your Dachshund does not take part in any of these activities, you can enjoy endless hours of fun together. He will love a game with safe toys and just clowning around or relaxing with his favorite playmate—you.

Your Dachshund will enjoy new experiences and endeavors with his favorite person, participating right along with him.

KEEPING THE DACHSHUND ACTIVE

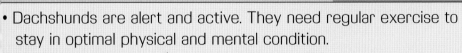

Overview

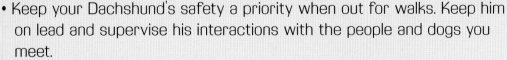

- Dachshunds are alert and active. They need regular exercise to stay in optimal physical and mental condition.
- Keep your Dachshund's safety a priority when out for walks. Keep him on lead and supervise his interactions with the people and dogs you meet.
- Dachshunds are versatile dogs, capable of participating in everything from bringing smiles and comfort as therapy dogs to competing against the most tenacious of dogs in an earthdog trial.

Your Dachshund and His Vet

Visits to the vet are much easier with a Dachshund than with a dog like an Irish Wolf-hound! You will be able to carry your Dachshund easily, either under your arm or in a crate. He might just bark at other visitors in the waiting room, but of course you will be a sensible owner and control this—at least I hope so!

Remember that, apart from being in strange surroundings, your Dachshund may be feeling a little off-color if he is not visiting just for a routine check-up, so make sure you take this into consideration.

"What's that you say? It's time to go to the vet?"

Because of the Dachshund's unique shape, back injuries can occur more easily than with other breeds. If you are visiting the vet with a back problem, take extreme care when lifting your dog. Ideally you should use a crate, in which movement is necessarily confined.

A healthy Dachshund is a happy Dachshund—and it shows!

It is sensible to make early contact with your vet, in part to build up rapport for any consequent visits. Obviously, if your puppy's course of vaccinations is not yet complete, you will need to take him to the vet in any case. Regardless of vaccinations, you should bring your puppy for a thorough exam within the first two or three days of bringing him home. If you do not already have a vet for other family pets, you should select carefully. Preferably take recommendation from someone who has dogs of their own, and whose opinion you trust. Location is also an important factor, for you must be able to get

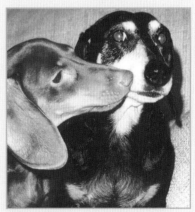

Senior citizens of the dog world need special love and attention from all of their friends, human *and* canine!

your dog to the vet quickly in an emergency and vet must be able to respond rapidly when needed. If you live in a rural area, please be sure that you choose a vet who has plenty of dealings with small animals. Many have a great deal of experience with farm animals but, sadly, their experience with dogs is limited, something I have learned the hard way in the past.

VACCINATIONS

The vaccines recommended by the American Veterinary Medical Association (AVMA) are called CORE vaccines, those which protect against diseases most dangerous to your puppy and adult dog. These include distemper (canine distemper virus or CDV), fatal in puppies; canine parvovirus (CPV or parvo), highly contagious and also fatal in puppies and at-risk dogs; canine adenovirus (CAV2), highly contagious and

high risk for pups under 16 weeks of age; canine hepatitis (CA1), highly contagious, pups at high risk. These are generally combined into what is often called a five-way shot. Rabies immunization is required in all 50 states, with the vaccine given three weeks after the complete series of puppy shots.

Non-CORE vaccines no longer routinely recommended by the AVMA, except when the risk is present, are canine parainfluenza, leptospirosis, canine coronavirus, Bordetella (canine cough) and Lyme disease (borreliosis). Your veterinarian will alert you if there is an incident of these diseases in your town or area so you can immunize accordingly.

The current American Animal Hospital Association (AAHA) guidelines recommend vaccinating adult dogs every three years instead of annually. Research suggests that annual vaccinations may

At your dog's annual checkup, the vet will give him an overall exam, including checking his heart, teeth and weight.

actually be overvaccinating and may be responsible for many of today's canine health problems. Mindful of that, the revised AAHA guidelines on vaccinations also strongly suggest that veterinarians and owners consider a dog's individual needs and exposure before they decide on a

Your Dachshund may like to tiptoe among the tulips, but be careful of what may be prowling about the garden. Dogs can fall prey to bug bites and bee stings just like we can.

vaccine protocol. Many dog owners now do annual titer tests to check their dog's antibodies rather than automatically vaccinate for parvo or distemper.

Your vet will advise you exactly about timing, when your dog can be exercised in public places after the course of vaccinations is complete and when boosters are due. Many vets now send reminder notices for boosters, but you should still make notes on your calendar. If overdue, it will probably be necessary to give the full vaccination program again. If you are visiting your vet for an initial vaccination program, do not allow your dog to come into close contact with other dogs in the waiting room, nor indeed the waiting-room floor!

Some people prefer not to subject their animals to routine vaccinations, but opt for homoeopathic alternatives. This needs to be carried out to the letter, so you must ideally be guided be a vet who also practices homeopathy. Also bear in mind that it will probably be difficult to find a kennel that accepts a dog without proof of a routine vaccination program.

PREVENTATIVE CARE

If your puppy was obtained from a truly dedicated breeder, all necessary care will have

tests for genetic abnormalities were carried out prior to the mating. A genuinely caring breeder will only have bred from a sound, healthy bitch and will have a selected a stud dog of similar quality.

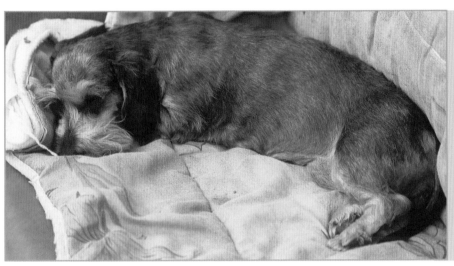

All dogs need to rest, but if your Dachshund shows signs of sleeping more than normal or otherwise acting like less than his perky, active self, contact your vet right away.

been provided not only for the litter but also for the dam. She will have had regular health checks and boosters, with a worming routine. These will stand her puppies in good stead and provide them with greater immunity than would otherwise be the case.

It is also of great importance that any recommended

CHECKUPS

When your Dachshund goes to the vet for his booster vaccinations, your vet will also give him a thorough physical examination. Your vet will check your dog's teeth and possibly do a tooth scaling, check his heart and check his entire body for problems not evident to the eye.

CHAPTER 14

NEUTERING AND SPAYING
Whether or not you decide to have your dog spayed is a matter of personal choice, but something I would never choose unless illness necessitated this. In any event, please never allow a vet to spay your bitch until after her first season. Timing "mid-season" will usually be advised.

Should you decide to opt for neutering your male dog or spaying your bitch, purely for the sake of convenience, you will have to take special care with subsequent weight control. In some cases, an aggressive or over dominant male can be easier to cope with after neutering, but this is by no means always so.

Obviously there are some reasons of ill health that necessitate such operations, particularly pyometra, which will usually require a bitch's ovaries to be removed. In the case of a male with only one or neither testicle descended into the scrotum, your vet may well advise castration to prevent the likelihood of cancer.

YOUR DACHSHUND AND HIS VET

Overview

- Once your Dachshund's vaccinations are complete, you will visit the vet annually for boosters and a checkup.
- Discuss the safest way to vaccinate your puppy and be diligent in keeping his scheduled appointments.
- One of the first things you and your pup will do together is visit the vet for an overall health check.
- Select a vet in whose ability you trust, who is conveniently located and with whom you can communicate well.
- Discuss the advantages and disadvantages of spaying/neutering your Dachshund with your vet.